Self-Discipline

The ultimate Guide On How to Be Happier, Become Productive an Achieve Goals by Self-discipline. Learn How change your mindset and avoid Procrastination.

Written By

James Foster

Table of Contents

INTRODUCTION

Thank you for purchasing this book!

Thank you for buying this book or even showing interest!

This book will explore the definition of overthinking and what you can do to change it. While going on a step-by-step path to alleviate the stress of overthinking and negative thinking processes, you can learn about the signs of overthinking and how it impacts your daily life.

Most people over-analyze situations in any aspect of their lives, whether it's their careers, relationships, lack of fulfillment, or a constant stream of tension. In a healthy life, all of these challenges seem unavoidable, and if you look around, people seem to have accepted that life and anxiety and depression will always be associated, even in the best-case scenarios.

Since the seminal book of Elaine Aron, The Highly Sensitive Human, was written in 1996, hundreds of thousands of HSPs (highly sensitive people) have begun to realize that their finely tuned nervous system does not render them defective for life. Approximately 15 to about 20 percent of the population has difficulty blocking out distractions, so noise, crowds, and time pressure may quickly overpower them.

The HSP appears to be particularly sensitive to pain, caffeine consequences, and violent movies. Highly sensitive individuals in their life are also made extremely anxious by bright lights, strong smells, and shifts. You will discover hundreds of new coping strategies in this companion book to The Highly Sensitive Individual to keep calm and quiet in today's over-stimulating environment, turning your anxiety into inner peace and joy. HSPs will consider growing up daunting in a culture that promotes violence and over-stimulation.

Enjoy your reading!

WHAT IS OVERTHINKING?

How many times have you heard a boss, co-worker, or a loved one say the words, "stop overthinking it" in the past? In the past, perhaps the question was addressed to you, and you responded with something like, "please explain what you mean," or "I don't know if you're thinking through it enough." a lot of times, communication is one of the major factors causing misunderstandings that happen between people in relationships. We are saying one thing, but it is understood differently. This complexity gets worse when we fall into the habit of overthinking, which simply takes in and processes more information than is necessary in order to complete a given task or find a problem. If we pull from a much broader range of information than is required for the things we're trying to do, whether it's something as easy as picking out the right tie or determining whether to break up with that new fiancé, we are all guilty of overthinking and most time make the task far harder on ourselves than it really needs to be.

All the thoughts running through your head hinder even the simplest tasks so avoiding distraction becomes almost impossible. Overthinking can lead to an emotionally damaging mindset, where you start thinking negatively about yourself, the people you love, or even the world. In your mind, too much negativity and anxiety will block out any possibility of positive thinking or finding the way to becoming a more optimistic, productive person.

I am happy to take this journey with you, and I know you are about to explore a lot of things about yourself as an individual. The simple fact is that from this book you have sought help is an important first bold step. Many people go on living with the chaos inside their minds throughout their entire lives while trying to find a pleasant existence. But we are going a lot more than that. We will be dropping the old chaotic mentality and seeking the road to understanding.

The book's title refers to finding a path through the disturbance within your mind but we're not going to just stroll around comfortably and leave the confusion where it is. Most people are very good at something called "compartmentalization," where people can deliberately store different thought processes in different parts of their minds, and train themselves to disregard one issue while focusing on another, in order to deal with many sources of stress, concern, and overthink. After a trauma, a lot of men and women experience this. To stop the sadness, they will focus on something that is positive, like their careers, and don't care about the suffering that needs to be worked through. Compartmentalization is an avoidance of the disturbing issue and although it can be beneficial in traumatic experiences, if we are to move past it, it is important to discuss what is happening in our minds. So, if you're ready, then let's get started!

CAUSES OF OVERTHINKING

There are a lot of things that cause overthinking, many catalysts that prompt overthinking which include bad habits that can lead to anxiety and excessive anxiety. These are not pleasant feelings, and they can easily turn into something much more serious and damaging what may seem like being simply careful and thinking things through.

At some point in our lives, we've all experienced worry. I remember when I was a kid, my mother would leave home very early in the morning to go to her workplace at the post office, and I would wake up just as she walked out of the door and felt a dire need to run to the front door and meet her so I could say bye and "I love you, mom." It didn't last or too long, but for a few nights, I was overcome by the fear that she would leave. It's easy to attribute to me as a young child, but let's think of another case.

You're a teenager and your elder brother heads out with his friends to Utah for a ski trip. He's just clocked 21 and you know there will be a lot of partying and drinking going on. Now you start to worry about all of the things that might happen. What if he gets involved in an accident driving around an unfamiliar environment? Would he be tempted to go drinking and driving? What if he slips and breaks a leg or an arm while skiing? What if he runs into a pool on the road and has a commotion and goes to a hospital and I don't get to know about it because he doesn't have his mobile device and well, that is an extreme example of acute worry, but I'm sure you get the idea what I'm talking about and you've experienced something similar about a loved one. Let's say you just watched a short clip on Twitter, Instagram, or Facebook where somebody ran right into a pool while skiing a couple of days ago. Now you've got this mental image to feed those concerns that run like a broken record through your mind. Maybe you have seen a report about a car accident caused by bad weather in Utah and now you have got that concern going through your mind.

The occasional spell of anxiety is perfectly normal, but when someone's life is consumed by constant anxiety about things that might happen without a good reason or justification, that person may be anxious. There are different kinds of anxiety but social and generalized are two of the most common forms. We may think of anxiety as a pathological form of overthinking and many people are experiencing such intense anxiety that they choose to take pills to relieve this feeling.

Generalized anxiety refers to everyday experiences that most people have no trouble getting through. Many people describe the feeling like a "concern for everything." Generalized anxiety affects everyday life and manifests as extreme fear and worry about things like leaving your home, going to the supermarket, the safety of the people you love, what's going to happen in the world, the possibility of war, whether you're eating right, whether you might be sick with serious illness and not realize it.

Some people are suffering from a specific phobia, but generalized anxiety appears to react at once to several different things, and can become unbearable. You may have suffered some sort of anxiety as you became conscious of the habit of overthinking. The first step to overthinking is to find out the triggers unique to you. There are a lot of causes to consider and you'll know when we talk about many of them, even if not all of them relate to you. Ideally, as you read this list, you will be able to identify which factors can play the greatest role in overthinking

Social expectation

To live and work in today's world is more demanding and challenging than ever before. Yeah, we have the new age conveniences that make life more comfortable and easy, but we also have to deal with the social life structure and the demand that we follow a timetable that fits something like this: education, more school, a career at the entrance level, ladder climbing, career at the senior level, retirement.

This has long been the norm for people living in economic-power countries. But over the last few decades, a lot has changed, and at a rapidly increasing rate. It is no longer so simple to find a job in a lucrative career that will be fulfilling and rewarding for thirty years or more.

Competition has risen alongside the people of the earth and the incredible technological advancement. Many of the job opportunities that were readily available to our parents no longer exist, and nowadays, you'd get a weird look for physically walking into a business and asking for a job application instead of making applications online. When you fail to get that dream job right out of college or high school, then the real fire trial begins. We could speak all day about office politics, competitiveness, and rivalry, but for now, let's concentrate on some of the key reasons to overthink in two of the most powerful realms of life: work and school.

We have started discussing the challenge of finding gainful employment in the modern age as a young adult, so let's continue to explore where overthinking can come into play here.

In the impact of globalization, advertising and marketing campaigns now dominate the world. You've been told from the very beginning of your career that you will have to contend with a lot of other candidates, many of whom may be more eligible than you. The interview process asks applicants to justify clearly why they should stand out above all the others. You should practice at home in front of a mirror, or think of all the likely questions that might arise. It's here when you can start thinking about how you are measuring up in your field next to others.

You've just earned a degree from college and at the time you started to feel like you were on top of the world with a million different prospects waiting for you (of course, best case scenario). Fast forward a couple of months, and you begin to realize that the job market is a bit more competitive than you ever thought, and you have not proven yourself to be a shoo-in to some of your dream organizations that have already passed you.

Many young people in the internet generation can attest to the challenges of graduating in the US during a recession and having difficulty finding any reasonable job at all, let alone starting a prestigious career in their fields. The weight of the social expectation that if you are smart and hardworking enough, you can and will get a great job opportunity becomes a big burden if and when things don't work out the way you'd imagine them in your school time. At this stage, you might start wondering if it's any fault or cognitive impairment within yourself that keeps you from your dreams.

The truth is, when it comes to securing or landing your "dream job," there are various factors at play, and sometimes working hard and a positive attitude are just not enough, despite all that your guardian or teachers informed you. This is why a lot of young adults continue the process of overthinking which is dominated by self-worth and adequacy issues. If society says I'm expected to be here or somewhere at this point in my life, that means I've not succeeded and there's something wrong with me.

Once that guilty verdict takes root, it's very tough to ignore the myriad images, advertisements, and slogans all around us that show the perfect professional man or woman in their lovely corner offices, clothed in the latest fashions, sharing how they made it through. This is when you start comparing yourself to other people's success, which simply adds to the problems going on in your mind that feed a sense of inadequacy and low self-esteem.

But let's just say you landed a decent job now. It's not a job you've always dreamed about, but it can be a good start to your career and you. Now it's time to show you really merit the job. You look around immediately at your boss, co-workers, and colleagues to see where you are on the ladder and how you're measuring up to your competition. Based on the type of personalities that surround you, you can feel a great good influence of pressure to do well and develop within the company.

Society made us know that the only way to grow and progress within your organization is to be the best, so professional life immediately becomes a rivalry. Every day this pressure will show itself as overthinking as you continuously evaluate how well you are doing your job. This in and of itself is really not a bad thing — everybody wants to be good at their jobs. A problem starts when we begin to compare ourselves obsessively with other individuals and when the job is no longer an atmosphere of several like-minded individuals working to build a better organization, but an intense competition to the top.

Once you manage to break into business society's top ranks, the rivalry turns toward other industries in your field — trying to overtake their market, forcing others out of the business, etc. And we've all heard of the expression that the more you win, the more you lose. This creates a whole new avenue of concern and overthinking as you evaluate how far you might fall if you make mistakes or fall off your ladder!

Aren't you? Do you feel constantly worried about where you are at work? You may be underemployed and feel bad, just as you have not gone far enough in life when you compete with others. This could be one of the most common causes of overthinking, but now it's time to move back in time to look at how social expectation takes a foothold in our minds as kids first. Let's take a look at the school's social expectations.

As children, most of us aren't actually thinking about what happens after school. We may have some far-reaching fantasies floating in our heads, but most of the time, we just want to know what mom has prepared for lunch today and whether that big kid will knock us off the swing at break today again. (Hopefully not, but you get the notion.) As we grew older and enter the middle and high school stage, social pressure and expectations were becoming in the immediate sense more central to our lives. We may think from a distance about our future careers, but most of us are concerned about whether or not students and teachers like us in school, the level of our popularity, whether or not we are going to get a date for a dance, etc. In this era, much of the social pressure revolves around physical appearance and either academic or competitive success.

Unfortunately, most girls begin to become worried about their physical appearance around this age, and may even begin to match this with their self-worth. The reason for overthinking has begun as these girls look around in social media and magazines at the beautiful models and career women and begin to compare themselves with those unrealistic ideals. Similarly, young boys may have an idol in sports or even a role model who has become very successful in their fields of work and begin to compare themselves as men, comparing their self-worth with academics or popularity or success in competitive sports.

The pressure only increases as we enter college, if that is your way forward. It's a struggle as many lose to balance a social life with academic life, leading to a situation whereby a student drops out of college. Staying focused and getting good grades, and that long-anticipated bachelor's degree gives passage into the realm of professional work, where a whole different world of social expectations and pressure awaits. As you've seen, much of our overthinking is what the professional or social environments can very well stem primarily from a wrong perception of ourselves in relation to others. The pressure starts early in life and continues as we are constantly surrounded by media images and texts dictating what success will look like and how it should sound.

Let's take a look at some more potential overthinking causes:

RELATIONSHIP

In romantic relationships, overthinking can vary from things like, "Does she really like me?" to "I just know he is coming home very late from work all the time because he's seeing another woman." Much of people's overthinking in relationships leads to incredibly traumatic sources of emotions such as envy and low self-esteem. Just as we are flooded with media images of "success," so are we obsessed with what it would feel like to be in a perfect relationship as well. A young teenage girl who is obsessed at high school about her looks may find it difficult later in a relationship because she considers other beautiful girls as constant threats. Young boys who are worried about making money can later face challenges in a relationship because he thinks that making money and working is of more importance than having a partner you spend quality time with.

Relationship overthinking can cause many problems and many of them can are capable of draining emotionally. When the thoughts that take over one's mind start clouding reality, you start a self-destructive cycle of negative emotions and feelings. Influences around the world have a way to get into our minds and we start to compare our relationships with those we see around us, on Twitter, Instagram, or Facebook.

This is a mistake because there is no single-size-fits-all system for how a happy relationship should work. You know when you get angry and upset about your partner you overthink because you feel he or she does not see you the same way some famous celebrities see their partner. Comparing your romantic life with that of others is an amazing way to miss out on what's special about you. I'm not saying you're supposed to ignore relationship issues. I mean, you should not attempt to compare those issues with the problems of others as a way to get them solved.

Each of us is special, and we all have different ways to deal with emotions and problems. Different doesn't mean it's wrong, but in a culture that covers the complexities of a relationship behind a perfect one's façade, people that encounter quite a harsh slap in the face once they move past the "honeymoon phase," and start to realize that it's not all the sweet and rosy in each other's faces. Relationships are not meant to be as simple and breezy as the couple makes it appear on all those advertisements of holiday resorts. Comparing and overthinking just complicates the challenge— when communication is the real necessity.

TRAUMA

Never a fun subject to broach, but if this is the cause of overthinking, it is a very important one. As mentioned earlier, we've all experienced some degree of worry about our own safety or that of our loved ones. We're concerned about our kids and their safety, about our partners and the health of our aging parents, etc. The problem comes up when these concerns become an ever-present cause of stress and anxiety— when overthinking becomes a chronic one.

After experiencing some kind of trauma a lot of adults are affected for the rest of their lives. Most times, one's parent's death will contribute to lifelong mindsets and perceptions that can impede an individual's vulnerability and ability to move beyond painful emotions. Abuse as a child is a big threat to the emotional well-being of an adult and typically needs to be addressed throughout the life of a person by treatments such as counseling. When trauma happens it causes the mind to be in a way that is very hard to forget or step beyond. As a result of this, the person may overthink through the lens of that trauma in terms of comparing or viewing other events throughout his life. For instance, a young girl being abused by an older male child may distort her ability to deal with men in the future without feeling things like fear, hate, or aggression.

These reactions include a much bigger threat to overall well-being. Most adults tend to compartmentalize as we spoke about earlier, or else totally forget or neglect the trauma until it grows up later in life suddenly. This is an illustration of what we call "thought suppression." most situations are too difficult to face, but many believe that the ongoing effort to endure this suffering would only lead to roadblocks in a person's life development. To put it another way, the pain must eventually be tackled.

On the overthinking level, past trauma develops thoughts and feelings about future events that have no relevance to the present. The fact that you were in a car when a fatal accident occurred and sustained terrible injuries as a teenager doesn't mean that every time you get into a car for the remainder of your life, you're likely going to get into another accident, but it feels like that. We let the impact and strength of those past emotions and anxieties flow into our life's events even before they happened. It's a trademark symptom of chronic overthinking in anticipation of something bad happening.

SOCIAL MEDIA

We are all familiar with the latest debate about how everybody gets into social media addictions. Without checking Facebook or our Twitter feeds, many people can't go for more than an hour without checking to see what's new and who liked our latest posts, etc. What you may not know is that social media addiction is a potent cause of overthinking. Throughout our lives, we have talked about such habits as comparing ourselves to others. Social media is one of the easiest ways to cultivate the habit

Looking at the Facebook page of a friend, there are odds, we see the beautiful, conceptually imposed perfect life they want those around us to see on the internet. We see pictures of people appearing off-the-cuff as they are. But most people take plenty of time to prepare their selfies, positioning themselves correctly. Most women put on makeup and then play around with the filters until they show the most perfect images they can see themselves. In the life of that person, you don't see the struggles and pressures, you just see the aspect they want you to see. It, once again, can lead many of us to compare our lives to the lives of others who seem better looking, more productive, wealthier, richer, etc. The negative feelings like jealousy and self-doubt are once again creeping up on us, just as they were when we were younger and compared to the queen of the prom or the captain of football.

All these things build up over time, and they may eventually take over, leading to overthinking a negative and self-destructive habit. Now that we've recognized some of the big causes for overthinking, let's look at the phenomenon that all of the internet surfing and Facebook scrolling contributes to information overload.

INFORMATION
OVERLOAD

Have you ever felt a feeling of burning out after being inundated with photos, text, and video from social media or news sites? Over the years, I've known a lot of people who admit that they sometimes spend a couple of hours a day, as many as 5 to 6 straight hours browsing the internet, reading the latest celebrity news, perhaps a few worlds new stories, scrolling all the Facebook feeds on their phones, watching the most trending YouTube videos or the most recent music videos from their favorite artists, reading all the nasty things online about dizzies between celebrities and politicians Your eyes may glaze over after a while, and feel like glass from taking all that information in.

Social media addiction is sort of a buzz term that has gained popularity as psychology and social science professionals observe the effects of social media on the minds of humans and society as a whole. We've been hopelessly addicted to the "present-ness" feeling that social media exposure can offer. When we read a new article about someone we find to be high profile, we feel like we're a part of something that's happening here and now that is important and urgent and full of kinetic energy.

The fact is, we do not really know those celebrities, even though they choose to share with us every single intimate detail of their daily lives. They want us to see only that part because that means they maintain an immense number of followers and can get rewarded for their exposure and access to huge markets by the big bucks. Such social media pioneers are dubbed "influencers," and the field is no longer limited to movie stars or multimillionaire girls and playboys. Now, we have a lot of niche groups that follow a particular individual in social media because of their attractiveness as role models in fashion, humor, or other facets of themselves that they have chosen to advertise successfully.

So why do I put this trend of social media up here? Okay, this is a great example of how we can bring about information overload by taking in a constant barrage of information from the internet. Although information overload has a very logical and reliable description of its impact on the brain, it can also be described through a discussion of how social media influences our inner lives and emotions, contributing to our overall sense of self and self-esteem in an unpredictable world.

Let's go down the rabbit hole on this line of thinking and see where we end up.

Our brains are complex to such a degree that we just begin to understand. The information that we carry in on a daily basis is largely forgotten and discarded soon after it has been processed. As we spend time on social media, we take in an infinite stream of information, which at the same time has a profound impact on the way we perceive and are discarded as useless information once we have seen it. As described above, when we read new information on social media that seems to happen now, we experience a high because everyone wants to have the feeling that they are part of the cutting edge of reality. Nobody likes to be the "last one to know" or, so to speak, to feel like we are behind the times. In a more general sense, we just feel bored a lot of time, and want some entertainment, right? Okay, let's dig a little deeper into this.

How can't those teens at the mall seem to be able to handle a single face-to-face conversation without having to check their phones every few minutes? Okay, that's part of the addiction to social media, for sure. But how did they form that addiction?

When we clutter up ourselves with this kind of information, we tend to need more and more sensory information to satisfy that desire and keep that high. With a bit of an experiment, you can feel this yourself.

If you know you're one of those people who enjoy checking out Facebook or Twitter or Reddit or anything else from time to time (or minute-by-minute) basis, take your mobile device from your purse or pocket or from where it's sitting next to you on the counter and put it in another room and make sure it's muted. Leave it there, and return to this book. Let's look a little later at how you feel. That may give you some insight into your own social media relationship!

Social media addiction is very much similar to drug addiction. That little sound that indicates we have a message on our phones activates the same areas of pleasure that some drugs activate in our brains. The more that we develop a routine and habit of going through our phones and feeding our brains with pictures and messages, the more our brain keeps asking us for more... and more. Ultimately we may get to a point where we get confused don't really know what to do with ourselves if our mobile phone breaks or dies or we lose it at a ceremony somewhere. The few hours or days without or mobile phone feel like a painful lack of connection from the world and from life.

But what is important to realize is that — it's all an illusion. Those sites and feeds on social media are designed to keep you wanting more and to keep you addicted. Marketing professionals know how long it takes to make those ads on Facebook that nestle in your feeds after you have bought something similar on another platform. Tabloid stories know how to formulate a story's title to get you to click it on and receive views that turn into dollars. Influencers know what their fans like and give them more about what keeps them coming back, whether it's beauty tips, parodies, comedy skits or famous celebrities, professional video game streams, etc. Everybody has something out there. It is a result of modern technology which is incredibly addictive and inevitable.

So what is so bad about information overload? We enjoy watching YouTube and keeping up with people's lives on Facebook, Twitter, or Instagram, what's so wrong with that? Okay, let's take a closer look at what's going on in our brains as a product of information overload, and how it can impact important aspects of our ability of decisions making.

INFORMATION OVERLOAD AND DECISION MAKING

Did you know that 25 percent of the work time for the average worker is spent handling email, according to a survey conducted by the McKinsey Global Institute? I'll be honest, I was not shocked when I first read this. Many of my mates are experts in different fields, getting hundreds of emails a week. Staying on top of that communication mountain sounds daunting to me, let alone at the same period trying to do your job. We talked about information overload with respect to social media, so I started with this subject because it could be the most open way to broach the topic. Now, let's look at information overload from a different perspective than many of us can relate to —information overload at work.

I personally can't imagine trying to sort through that huge amount of emails in the email scenario, particularly if half of them expect an answer. But let's go ahead and add to that situation. You work in an office, getting hundreds of emails a day, but your job often dictates that you respond to the phone all day long, guiding each caller to the correct number, answering business questions, etc.

In addition, you are supposed to go through a large stack of documents to fill out the financial information and payment forms for clients. It sounds like pretty much the work, right? Let's assume that at first you're very overwhelmed, but eventually you'll find a way to handle all that stuff. And you know what? It feels great. It feels great to feel like you are able to handle so much of a workload and walk out with your dignity at the end of the day. But... how much dignity have you left at the end of the day? There could be something that you don't even know yet. The abundance of information has a cumulative impact on our decision-making ability. And we don't even know much of the time that it's happening.

As a teenager, I used to work in a coffee shop and one of the things I prided myself on was my multitasking ability. Finally, I started working alone for long shifts, managing customer lines that sometimes reached out the door and down the hallways! I soon learned to work very, very fast. I'd juggle with making beverages and managing cash like some kind of ninja food service. I was very proud of that too. I felt like I really worked hard and achieved something that needed ability and finesse. For sure it does. The problem was that after a while I began to notice "burnout" signs, which is the eventual outcome of information overload associated with persistent multitasking.

Just like burnout from watching too many YouTube videos at once, the pressure I was putting on the processing power of my brain was getting too much. This burnout shows itself at a certain point in making mistakes. Maybe I get tired towards the end of my shift and make an incorrect adjustment for a customer who then gets really frustrated, exacerbating and turning physical and mental tiredness into emotional tiredness. You could start to see where that is heading. Information overload leads to burnout leading to poor decision-making, even when we don't even tend to know it is happening.

We're all familiar with the picture of a "workaholic," an individual who seems to work tirelessly, obsessed with the idea of being a perfectionist at the works they are given to do, never taking a break. What we know very soon is that this isn't acceptable, either as an observer or as the workaholic himself. Our brains finally start to send out signs of exhaustion. We can either agree at this stage that we need to slow down or ignore the warning and continue to work. This is the situation where bad decision-making comes into play.

Bad decision-making can apply to many different things, not just about work, but about our relationships with others. As discussed earlier in this book on causes of overthinking, when it comes to our personal lives, an inundation of knowledge about how a relationship will look can lead to poor decision making and belief systems. At some point, it becomes very difficult to move outside of the knowledge with which we have filled our minds in order to clearly see our own circumstances.

As the rate at which people show, many people like to start with a belief that they know what a person wants and needs, and then somewhere down the relationship track, that changes Are that change affected by what we see in relationships with other people? Those unrealistic and doctored portrayals of social media joy and perfection? Personally, I assume that there is a good chance that this will at least play a significant role in the eventual breakup of many relationships that might have begun on a high note. It's not unreasonable to assume that in a society that advertises the message that "you're worth it" to people and that you should never at any point in your life settle for less than the American dream— a beautiful relationship to a beautiful, sexy spouse, great kids, massive house, dream job, and a decent car— the challenges of a real relationship prompted some to abandon. Maybe we decide there is only someone else out there to give us the flawless, easy, uncomplicated life we see in TV shows.

But that's certainly not the case. Real relationships are taking real-time, not just the right shampoo or hundred-dollar facials a month.

Many decisions made in the heat of information overload have more serious and long-lasting effects than others. Our minds are trying to draw essential information in the midst of information overload to make a decision from a massive pool of irrelevant and extraneous information. The probability of making bad decisions rises with the pace at which those decisions are expected to be made.

For instance, if you have just three seconds to decide which exit to take on the highway and you have GPS on your mobile phone, radio blaring in your ears, kids shouting in the back seat, and police car speeding with the siren blaring, you definitely do have a lot more trouble making this decision than if you were driving alone, radio on a low level of music volume, and you've already determined from home the exit you will be using. The brains are not always distinguishing vital information from non-vital information as we want it to be. This information overload can easily turn nasty if a driver makes a wrong decision and gets upset. Emotions, like irritation, are now involved, and this only increases the severity of information overload, contributing to poorer decision-making

Consider an air traffic controller in a more professional setting, who is responsible for many aircraft coming in at the same time. Ideally, each employee is skilled and used to manage such a workload, but within a split second, one bad decision resulting from information overload will affect hundreds of people's lives.

The message is clear: information overload can result in poor decision-making which has impacted not only our lives but the lives of several people.

Now that we understand how information overload impacts our brains let's think about some strategies to help pull us out.

Moving away from information overload

As you have probably realized in your life by now, there is no complete removal from the tornado of information overload happening that seems to flood into every area of modern life. But there are methods to move away from information overload by slowly getting rid of the sources of those triggers in your life.

The first step is always to understand that this influx of information in some way negatively impacts your life. Whether it is a negative feeling, such as low self-esteem, or a performance problem at work, you've realized that overloading your brain has weakened your ability to distinguish what your emotional and physical energy is worth and what isn't.

How do you feel you know that you are away from your phone for a couple of minutes? Did you forget to put it away? And did you fight an urge to get up and check it out? Either of these responses is good, due to the fact that now, you know a little bit more about how inadvertently or actively addicted you might have become to your mobile phone and whatever applications you continue to use constantly all day.

One of the greatest things you can do to get this ball rolling is to stick to keeping your phone time-limited every day. Even if at first it's just a little bit, do your best to substitute the time you spend surfing through the internet on your phone with other things — activities that don't require a computer. Go outside your house and take a stroll, listen to some lyric-free soft music, play with your cat or dog or whichever pet you have, or get one of those interesting adult books.

You can also limit your multitasking. This sounds like I tell you to take things easy or to work less. It is not about promoting laziness. You will find that the more you commit to working on one task at a time the higher the quality of your work output will. Instead of getting a lot of things done at a time with a normal or below-standard result, you'll accomplish an assignment and even surpass your own standards of what you thought you couldn't beat.

Make an actual phone call and find out time to go to a quiet restaurant or perhaps your own home to meet a colleague for coffee. Commit to doing away with each other's cell phones, muted and face-to-face conversation. Try to avoid media subjects, and explore more important issues. Ask about his or her welfare, and how they feel. You can end up forming connections that you have not made in years.

During work take a break at least once in an hour from your office to stroll around, free your mind and stretch your legs. This may seem to have nothing to do with information overload, but working on many activities over a long period of time appears to divert our focus from physical health. Sitting is not healthy for our bodies and it helps to move around a lot, even for just a few moments, at least once every hour. If it's a nice day, take a walk around the workplace, go get a beer, or walk around the compound. You're going to be surprised at how much better you're going to feel and it's like giving your mind a reset in the midst of likely information overload.

Lastly, take a break from all those tales of doom and gloom which are published in the news nonstop. I mean, it's a good thing to stay informed about what's happening in our country, but you can overdo it. News media can be as addictive as social media and overloading yourself with such information can cause information overload as quickly as possible. It is extremely important to monitor continuously where your news information is coming from. Be careful about whom you want to follow, and from which sources of news you choose to get your information. Investigate the facts they give, and see if they are in line with what you think. Cross-referencing details with other sources of news, and see if they match. It's not an easy thing to do but you can take measures to protect yourself from sources of news that are less than credible.

Now that you have made steps towards eliminating sources of information overload in your life, it is time to address the issue of the overload that is already there. We'll be talking about how to declutter your mind in the next chapter to make room for a whole new outlook on life.

DECLUTTER YOUR MIND

You know where some of the greatest overthinking causes are, you are working to slowly eradicate or reduce the issues that lead to information overload in your life, and now it's time to address the confusion inside your mind.

The concept of clearing your mind to be able to focus on the objectives of life or the daily tasks has become very popular in recent years. Several authors and speakers have provided plenty of information and advice on how people can begin organizing, assessing, and then eliminating unwanted clutter from their minds. I agree that analyzing and knowing what is troubling your mind is an important first step in that process. That way, you will start connecting certain sources of overthinking with the thoughts that run through your mind. Cleaning up the overthinking sources is just as critical as eliminating the brain's individual thoughts.

Note that, human beings are programmed to take information in and process it. Most of this information is stubborn, inducing emotional responses that can't just be pressed and dragged like on our computers to the recycling bin! Falling into a routine and making real progress in clearing your mind and learning how to manage and measure the importance of thoughts and feelings as you continue living your life will take some time and concentration.

This journey is the beginning of a lifelong and life-changing process. Just because you are now discarding irrational thinking, it doesn't mean that in the future it will never try to creep on you again.   Trust yourself, and your ability to never stop moving forward.

So what do I mean to declutter the mind when I say it? Simply stated, there's no way you can start developing better habits and more positivity without first cleaning off the thoughts that hamper your progress.

Most feelings and repetitive thinking patterns are connected to emotions that hold us back and even block our perceptions of what is actually happening. We've already discussed how external influence and emotional pain can manifest in a distorted view or assessment of a loved one, a coworker, parent, or even a kid.

Many people take so much of the world's negative information that they lose all sense of confidence or respect for people, even strangers! Of course, when it comes to finding and forming real connections with other people this is seriously restricting. Individuals who automatically start distrusting and disrespecting others will inevitably isolate themselves, leading to even more mental anxiety and depression.

The fact that loneliness and depression are related in many ways is attested to by most psychologists. Human beings, from the time we are born to the day we die, are social animals. For a long time, we are reliant on our carers. Once we become self-sufficient, we rely on others to work together to keep us alive. Society may look much different now than it did so many decades ago, but from our relation and connection with other human beings, we still derive pleasure and an important fulfillment in life.

I mention those points because, I believe, a cluttered mind is certainly a form of loneliness. Speak of yourself as buried beneath an enormous pile of thoughts that actually have little impact on your life course. What was it that cardi b said this week?   I should get the recipe I've seen on Facebook for that dinner. I can't believe that Drake has said that again. Is my tummy too big? How do I lose weight as do the celebrities? Was my boss angry at me for the joke I said at lunch today... blah, blah, blah.

Those thoughts may or may not ring any bells in your head, but I bet you will see a trend if you sit down and think really about many of the thoughts that keep coming back to you. You'll also see that in terms of your performance or progress in life, these thoughts or this sequence of thoughts really do nothing for you.

To our view, many of these crowding feelings are examples of what marketers want you to think about. When you worry about something in your life or yourself so often, you may be tempted to buy goods that offer immediate improvement. It is important to distinguish which of your normal thought processes originate from you, and the ones that originate from the outside like a Facebook ad or Twitter trend. In the last chapter, we talked about thinking and sorting in terms of your information overload. Now we will start talking about a similar process, only that we are going to discuss the cluttered thoughts that are already in your mind.

Effects of a cluttered mind over time

We discussed in detail in previous chapters that marketing-based information overload can result in negative feelings and emotions to yourself and others. The marketers are hoping to turn this negative emotional response into an incentive for buying their products to fix those problems.

So now, let's take a more detailed look at how a cluttered mind and information overload can have an effect on the brain over time.

You may have been informed that the new work colleague at the office, let's call her Jessica, boast about her brilliance in multitasking. She seems to fly easily through her tasks in a single morning and finish them quickly, while others find it difficult to complete one or two tasks before the lunch break in the organization. Jessica may get the impression that she gives her mind four, five, or even six different tasks, and her brain moves through all these duties in a timely and effortless manner at once. Okay, I just got to tell you. Jessica is just... wrong!

The human brain can just focus on one thing at a time. This is it. A person can learn to move with lightning speed from a thing to another, but he still concentrates only on one thing at a time. Basically, what a brilliant multitasker comes down to is, Jessica does a lot of things in a short period of time, devoting very, very little time to every particular job. Therefore, the problem becomes one of quality versus quantity.

This kind of rapid movement from one task to the next, depending on the type of job, maybe even a concentration that allows one to do the same work over and over without getting too frustrated of it can be beneficial. Factory workers are required, during their shifts, to perform the same role again and again. To keep up with such a demand, you need a steady concentrated mind, or else he or she might dose off!

While Jessica appears to be doing a great job, the truth is that her "multitasking" raises her chances of making a mistake. When this happens, it can lead to personal frustration, because up to this point, Jessica has judged her performance based on how much she is doing — not really bothered about the quality of the work she's doing. Especially in today's extremely competitive environment, one error at work can lead to a lot of emotional frustration, which is brought home and turns into tension from one place to the next. This is a common symptom of a cluttered mind. This happens when you can't stop worrying about work, even if you are eating dinner with your children at home, then you're losing out on some of life's greatest joys— spending quality time with your children.

If you are, don't get discouraged. It is quite common, and there are certainly ways of handling this. But for now, let's cover some more explanations on why a cluttered mind is harmful over time.

Just as we discussed information overload in the previous chapter, too much information results in poor decision-making. If we lower the burden or remove this overload trigger entirely, we will begin to see how the emotions already in our minds are influencing us at present. Just think of it. How long ago did you become fascinated with this or that area of your life? If you have already found a cause of overthinking your childhood or teenage memories, the answer is a very long time!

When our thoughts ring back themselves and contribute to the chaos that is already filling our brains, it becomes more difficult to discern between what good habits are and what is bad in terms of processing of thought. You would assume, for example, that a general attitude of mistrust, even at work, protects you against possible threats or risks. But look deeper and look at the flip side of that argument— what do you miss out on? And do you feel happy or unhappy about that attitude? Decluttering your mind is all about doing away with those thoughts that negatively affect you. The results can be mental, physical, psychological, etc. How emotions can do to you over time is breathtaking.

The harmful coping strategies

Most people who understand negative thinking processes but don't know how to deal with them transform into unhealthy ways of coping which can lead to serious problems in health. Drinking, smoking, and illicit drugs are just a few of the most popular. How many times in a drama series have you seen the main character demonstrate she wants a cigarette to deal with the stress of a situation?

Perhaps, after something terrible happens, a character who appears to have quit smoking sneaks out into the patio for a quick smoke. When it comes to dealing with a cluttered mind, these quick remedies do much more harm than good. It may feel so good to forget about them in the meantime, but they will never really go away without resolving your thoughts and behaviors and you will need stronger and stronger measures of your coping strategy to send those thoughts away.

Another way that people try to run off their own brains is by coming home and tuning out in front of the television screen. It feels great to come home from a hard day at work and, instead of addressing the issue you've had with your manager or talking to your spouse about making a significant and stressful decision, you literally plop down on the sofa to binge on a Netflix series you've always wanted to see. Once more, the action is only preventative, not a remedy. Those problems will still need to be tackled once that binging session is over, even though running away for a short time felt good.

Yet, beyond just running away, think about the quality of a life filled with thoughtless, annoying behavior. What do you really grow towards? What are your intent and meaning? Definitely not vegging out eating junk food every night. Decluttering your mind means returning to your real-life ambitions, interests, desires, and beliefs.   There they are, covering all the confusion inside. So let's make it clear so that we can get to the good part!

Let's declutter

The brain can perform just one task at a time, as I have said. So to analyze a group of disturbed thinking processes in your mind, we need to take some time to note down all those thoughts that we would find unhelpful, negative, hurtful or irritating. Note, it's not always about just shredding a thought that negatively affects us — sometimes we need to weed these out and tackle them directly to dissipate their powerful influence.

Once you've got a list before you, it's time to take a look at each and feel how that thought affects you. The key to eliminating a negative thinking process is to commit to disrupting the thought whenever it comes into your mind. If you start thinking about that woman you think yesterday was flirting with your husband, stop the welling up resentment and ask yourself, "Has my husband ever given me the basis to believe he'd cheat me?" How often does he say that I love you all day long?" Would a dialog about the feeling get rid of the insecurity that I feel inside?" Most times, a brief conversation can be all it takes for profoundly hurtful feelings to be helped. Remember, it's your choice in life. If you really are in a relationship where your partner is continuously in question, then it is time to take the bold step on what to do about it. Before you agree, do not just wallow in intense grief for another 10 years.

Looking at each item in your list, write down one positive feeling in another column next to it that would essentially eliminate the negative emotion-related to that bad thinking. For instance, if you think incessantly about how well you're doing your job and fear you're not good enough, imagine achieving a challenging task and calling your supervisor to the office to applaud you.

Maybe it's hard to focus on good things happening all around the world because every source of news you read only talks about the disasters. Do some research and check out for something amazing that's been happening in the world lately. It may not be part of the top headlines, but I promise you there are always beautiful people doing great work in the world. In this case, the interruption task is to start thinking about the good thing you've figured out every time your mind wants to go to the bad thing that has happened that week. It's not about downplaying what's happening in the world— it's about strengthening your mental state so you can get back into being a positive and satisfied person. Getting sinkholes sapping the positive energy in your mind is not beneficial for anyone.

If you get the hang of this method, go ahead and continue until you finish two columns in your list. The negative thought patterns are represented in one panel, the opposite one covers an interrupting thought process to combat it.

I wish I could say that just writing down this stuff would automatically dissipate your cluttered mind, but you're going to make a commitment to stay mindful all day long so you can stop those negative or cluttering feelings. Some of those thoughts might just clutter your mind, not be linked to negative emotion. In this scenario, the interruption technique will be to completely disregard the idea when it comes into the mind. Finally, having eliminated sources of information overload should go a long way towards getting rid of the simple irrelevant thoughts.

Let me tell you, if you've tried to tackle all the cluttering thoughts you can think of in your head, you've certainly come a very long way from the state you were in a couple of hours ago. At first, it may be difficult but as you practice this routine disruption of cluttering and negative thoughts, you will soon begin to see the positive changes. It will become faster, and ultimately automatic.

Indeed the brain is quite versatile. Scientific research has studied the brain's trait, called neuroplasticity, in recent years. If you substitute negative thoughts with positive thoughts, the brain is literally rewired! Take that, Jessica.

Now that you start moving beyond the thoughts that had cluttered your mind for years, perhaps even decades, it is indeed time to move on to something much more interesting.

Finding your real goal, purpose, passion, or goal

It's been defined in different terms in a lot of different ways— our purposes for living or the best part of living. We wake up every day for our thoughts or emotions or desires to pursue our goal. Maybe we get a lot of joy from practicing just a hobby. Whatever you want to explain, now is the time to begin to think thinking about how to fill that empty space, where your mind's cluttered thoughts once took root. It's time for a further exercise in thinking.

Think back to when you were a kid or perhaps a teen. Was there anything in your life that brought you childhood joy? Was there a sport or a talent or a hobby that you have been perfecting most or all of your leisure time? You may have enjoyed reading and just reading lots and lots of books each year during summer break. Do you enjoy diving, above all? Would you play basketball or baseball? Horse riding? Sketching and drawing? Maybe just chatting and laughing with friends was what you looked forward to doing each and every day. Whosoever it was, I want you to bring back the memory, if possible, to a time when you were doing all that you wanted to do. How did that make you feel? Do you remember the joy that it gave you?

Most people struggle with this fallacy that when we become adults the happiness that we feel in childhood disappears forever. This cannot be any further from the facts. Each of us still has that kid inside them, and once we reach a certain age, it's not a necessary phase of life that we abandon that. Most people have gotten a successful and fulfilling career from their childhood passions. We relive the joy that we felt every day as a child, only now, they get paid for it!

We don't have to give up being a child's independence of mind, playfulness, enthusiasm, excitement, all the most precious bits just because we are now adults. I want you to remember the things that made you excited as a child because now is the time to figure out how to make that happiness manifest in your life. I'm not referring to trying to relive the past or become a child. What I'm saying is adults will experience joy and excitement just like a child. It is just culture and other cluttered minds that tell us there is no place for such things. Let's prove their point wrong!

Get that paper out once again, maybe just turn over the sheet you used to work on the previous exercise. Creating a list of the things you liked to do as a kid might be helpful at first. Maybe go and find some old home movies or photos from your dance rehearsal or scout boys troop, etc. Take some time to note just how much happiness these things have brought you. Just think about things you love to do now. When was the last time you had some free time to pursue something you enjoyed doing? If it's been a long time, you might need to think a little longer about what you like to do. Don't be deterred. You can always choose something you'd like to know about, perhaps this will turn into your new hobby!

Write down a few things you'd really like to concentrate on as a strategy to bring happiness and relaxation of childhood back into your life. There may be a lot of things you derive joy in doing but not exhausting yourself is crucial. Many people won't be able to just leave their jobs and start following their full-time interests (wouldn't that be fun!), so let's pick one or two things you'd like to incorporate into your life.

The last thing you would do is turn your passion into a chore, so when I suggest making out some time to devote to your happiness, I think you can try to prioritize doing things just for you every day. That might be as simple as taking a nap! Finding out spare time for yourself is a perfect way to work with the interruption strategy that we discussed earlier to reinvent how the brain interprets your everyday life. When you wake up each and every morning with the inner fear in your gut of having to wake up and drive to work daily, then this experience is familiar. It may seem like a task that is not achievable now, but I guarantee you will have discovered, by the end of this book, the essential steps to take towards understanding a productive and fulfilled daily life.

If you are someone like me who needs guidance, start by finding and taking courses that are related to something that you have wanted to learn or try.

If it's been a couple of years since you drew something and used to enjoy drawing, find a private classroom, maybe a community classroom in your area, and you may just find some friends with like minds! You will find that the more professional growth you seek, the more naturally you will find what makes you happy. Once you've learned to be conscious of your thinking processes, because there were too many thoughts in the way, you would eventually start to notice things you hadn't thought of before.

DECLUTTER YOUR ENVIRONMENT

Did you ever see this coming (before looking through the outline of this book)? You may ask, what does my overthinking have to do with a clean home? Well, the answer is -it goes a long way!

In reality, our environments affect us in significant ways that are not always visible and felt immediately. An employee who has to perform his duties in an unpleasant atmosphere would undoubtedly be underperforming when compared with another employee in a clean and comfortable environment.

Think about the way look (hopefully you've performed this at least once or twice!) after a thorough cleaning of your house. Doesn't it feel good to look around both your compound and interior and see a clean home? This raises the spirits and clears the mind, just like the physical space before healing you. Sometimes, the clutter in our environment can have a direct influence n our minds ' clutter. Let's get ready!

Keep in mind that this is not yet another one-size-fits-all solution. When it comes to home management, every person has a different body type, style, and level of comfort, and having a clean home does not necessarily guarantee a huge performance boost. The truth is, you can only change your attitude by decluttering your home, so why not make that effort?

If you're living with a friend, loved one or roommate, you're going to want to discuss this strategy before you just push it all around or throw it away! If it's a common living room it should be a collective effort. There is a good possibility that your living partners will be on board after you explain to him or her what you'd like to do!

But first, let's look into why reorganizing and decluttering one's home can be vital.

In the last chapter, we addressed how people with distracting or unhealthy behaviors can try to avoid overthinking. Well, being untidy and disorganization are good indications there are certain issues in the mind that need to be addressed and organized. Sometimes, our external environment is a representation of the world in our mind

Look at your house or your personal place of living. How do you feel about the way it looks now? Does that leave you feeling sad? Overwhelmed? Most times, our lack of discipline, when it begins to feel like we cannot manage it, can get out of hand. Trying to address the external consequences before addressing the internal effects of overthinking, fatigue, anxiety or depression is always counterproductive. If you're not tackling the cycle of thought and bad habits, then even if you endeavor to clean up your environment, there's a possibility it will start to look just like it did in days or even weeks before.

If you've seen the Hoarders television show, then you realize that much of the behavior of a hoarder has to do with the emotional connection to some form of traumatic experience going on in their lives. If this is you and you have taken steps to improve the way your thought is processed, then you are in a strong position to start discussing your personal living room.

Keep in mind that this method is mostly applicable to those of us who need help with something that has become something of an overwhelming mission. You may have no issue with keeping your home clean and tidy, and that's fantastic. My advice for those of you who can be identified this way would be to think about adding another dimension into your home that will foster relaxation and comfort. Maybe you can pay attention to a small plant during the week, or you can put a plaque with an inspirational quote on the wall where you'll see it each and every day. Any kind of little reminder you can offer yourself every day as you move on your journey can be an enormous boost to your confidence.

But if you're one of many who thinks you have a huge task on your hands, let's get started from the outset.

The first thing is to step back and accept that you must take one step at a time. Don't look at the entire building, and feel discouraged that you can't organize anything. You have to start with a single room, perhaps even the smallest space

Look all over this room, and reflect on how it got this dirty and why it's there. Does just looking at your things cause you a twinge of discomfort or sadness? If so, then that will certainly be tackled.

You'll need a couple of different boxes or bags because different things are meant for different futures. Finding someone there you trust can be helpful in helping you determine which one is.

One box should be marked donation and these are the items that you don't need in reasonably good shape. It's not about making use of it in the future, or not. If it has been sitting there for a long time, and you haven't seen it, there are possibilities, you wouldn't need it again. Please, dispose of it.

You will also be in need of a trash bag. Even when we have developed negative emotions associated with attachment, it can feel difficult to let go of stuff we have been hanging on to for so long. When decluttering your environment, think about your goals. Weigh the value of this or that thing in your life against what you are trying to achieve. If the emotional reaction connected to that item falls into your life journey's category of the hindrance, then you must get rid of it. When you can't bring yourself to the garbage or donate anything, perhaps someone you know can keep it for you. Yet holding on to it just keeps holding you back.

A third, fourth, and perhaps fifth box for those items you hold and need to arrange should be included. Perhaps in this room, there is something that will make more sense in another room, etc. Until reorganizing these things, you'll want to get all up from the floor or out of the room so that after dusting the ceiling corners to get rid of cobwebs, ceiling fans, and blinds, you can properly dust or sweep the floors and wipe down the tables or other surfaces throughout the space n the room. You'll consider organizing and redecorating the space a lot more fun once it's nice and clean!

That is the cycle that you are going to follow for the rest of your room. Take a break if it starts to get stressful. You don't have to do all that in a single day. Keep remembering what a big and important step you are taking to make your life better

Areas such as the kitchen and bathroom may be the most demanding. When attempting to clean surfaces, remember to remove and arrange objects as this will just frustrate you and contribute to a suboptimal level of cleanliness. If you are financially okay, you might consider hiring a professional cleaning service to come in to clean just a few of the house's most demanding rooms. If they are really dirty, then don't feel embarrassed. Just be sure to remove and discard any things you need to be out of the way. Most services can offer great complimentary rates and one-time service packages for new customers.

There are many ways to dispose of things that you have known are not required or used. I already listed donations. Donation boxes can be sold at shops such as Goodwill or the Salvation Army. If you have things like kids' clothes or toys, maybe there is a church you should donate to. Another option is a yard sale. Make a little cash for those things and rest assured that somebody else can make good use of them.

MINIMALISM

I would like to introduce a principle and lifestyle which has become increasingly popular in recent years. I'm not saying anyone reading this book should instantly get rid of 90 percent of their things and follow this lifestyle, but I think it's going to open your mind to the potential and positive mindset that minimalism cultivates to discuss this subject.

Minimalism is a simple concept, very basic. Professionals strip down to the bare necessities of life in order to convert to the easiest and most natural lifestyle.

You may have heard of a movie on Netflix released in 2015 entitled Minimalism: A Matt D'Avella Directed Documentary about the Important Things. It is a great introduction to this movement and if you are interested in understanding more I highly recommend it.

The belief systems and the motives for switching to a minimalist lifestyle differ from person to person. Many have other traditional beliefs and values, such as taking care of their environments and minimizing their own "ecological footprints" on earth. Most professionals are young adults who have "burned out" (sound familiar?) in our current professional and career economic rat race and who have simply turned to a drastic attention transfer after discovering that they did not like the direction they were going in.

This realization is similar in many ways to the realization you may have had before starting to read this book— that your present way of living with an overcrowded, overthinking mind is an epitome of what you want out of existence, or of your ambitions, or of your happiness, or all these things combined together. A move away from the overly materialistic, chaotic, exhausting lifestyle of non-stop gain is a transition to minimalism. It is a rejection of all these things surrounding you that shapes a cage and addiction for more.

As we remove items that have emotionally imprisoned us, like a junkie who decides to make a change and get rid of unwanted stuff, a huge wave of liberation and clarification awaits us to claim Minimalism is perhaps the best example in terms of how what is going on inside our minds can match what is going on in our immediate surroundings. It can almost be represented as a spiritual practice in which you dedicate yourself for the rest of your life to maintaining the mentality of clarity and presence every day. Around you, the simple lifestyle is a constant reminder of the mental changes that have occurred.

Of course, money is one of the most powerful addictions in modern society. If I were to take a guess, I would assume that your initial list of overcrowding thoughts contained financial concerns, likely near the top. And that does make sense, right? Today, surviving without money is difficult. And everything is steadily costing as we get older, and the more we get. Those investments that were meant to bring us comfort and independence turn out to be money traps — like our cars. Some people feel that they need the largest SUV on the market to suit their urban lifestyles without children... ok, I may get off track. But do you see where I am heading?

The mindset that needs more, more, more attitude leads to nothing but boredom, uncertainty, depression, and an exhausted mind affected by all trying to tell us what we need. If we had only the latest iPhone version, all our problems would just go away! I'd look prettier if I changed my hair and had highlights and life would be simpler! If I can get the job and work longer hours, I'll be happier and healthier! Could go on the list forever.

Now the mentality behind minimalism is getting clearer. It's not just a matter of getting rid of things to save money, though this is a bonus. It's about freeing your mind from the chaos that life throws at you— things that are wrongly thought to bring the things that are found only in personal relationships and interactions, reflection imagination, belief systems, etc.

Money can't buy happiness, actually. Happiness itself is a fluid thing that naturally happens out of encounters in personal life that rarely have much to do with money.

So how serious is that stuff going about minimalism? Okay, if you're interested, there's a whole new world of what's recognized as "tiny houses" which is gaining popularity. Okay, I'm sure this is probably way too extreme for you at this point but checking out if you're interested is still a fascinating thing.

Small homes are just that— quite, very small. These can be as small as your bathroom and only provide the very bare minimum of modern conveniences. You have a place to sleep, a place to prepare simple meals, maybe a small area to store very, very few belongings and... That's it! But when you look into it, it's not all that far from living on RV, which is another very common way to gain freedom from the modern world's stresses and financial strain. (An RV doesn't give much more than a tiny home— plus, it's mobile!)

The idea is that people don't really need all that stuff advertisers are telling us they need. In fact, we can live on a very simple diet of good, safe, environmentally friendly food and the joy of being around our loved ones. Applying this theory to your own life could help you see how trivial and unimportant many of your past worries and concerns were. We are conditioned to feel emptiness, and feel the need to fill that void with things. When those things start to clutter our homes and personal spaces, we can see a direct parallel within our minds between this world and what goes on inside us.

Decluttering your home and making way for a fresh start is important in helping your mind's effort to declutter. Take the time you need to achieve this important step and you'll soon be ready to build on the new and better you.

Once you've taken steps to declutter your house, you'll find that you're not only able to move about your room more easily, but also that your thinking is becoming clearer! For a reason, all these measures are included together and will work well for you as you advance.

Look around your home once you have reached this place, and take a deep breath. This is your new canvas designed to create your life the way you have wanted to live it.

The next step on our journey is to start focusing on how to shape good habits that will sustain your continued victory over overthinking and information overload Some people never get to this point so give yourself a big pat on the back. This may also be a good time to reflect on the people you're very close to in your life. Have you got a loved one or a close family friend who seems to be in the same boat that you have been in terms of information overload and overthinking? You might be able to recruit a partner to help you develop good habits while you're working. You might just be dramatically changing another life in the process along the way!

DECENT HABITS

It's not enough to concentrate on getting rid of the bad habits alone. Now, good habits need to be incorporated into our new life. I hope for all those unneeded or negative feelings, you have continued to work on the interruption of those bad thoughts.

You even have a new activity coming up to try or go back to when you were a kid. It is time to concentrate on you as a person, and what you want out of your life. You can do several things regularly to prime your mind, body, and spirit for the renewed you. Let's dig at some of those.

PRIORITIZE YOUR RELATIONSHIP WITH

PEOPLE, NOT THINGS

In today's information-saturated world, taking out our phones whenever there is some amount of downtime has become normal. Looking at people waiting in lines throughout the area, in shops waiting to eat in restaurants, they're either sitting or standing with their heads down, nose in their mobile phones

And why can't they? We can play fun games on our phones, chat with colleagues and friends, read news articles or news stories, keep up with our entertainers... Wait a second, did we not just talk about getting rid of the information overload? That's Okay. Now it's time to make your relationships and connections with others a priority.

Let's present you with a small challenge to try this week.

Leave your mobile phone in the car when you go to the grocery store or bank, or maybe even when you take your family out for dinner next time. What?! Indeed, I said that. Leave your smartphone in your car. When you stand in queue— and this may be a bit nervous — try to say something positive to the person behind or before you. I know... you might get a confused look, maybe they're going to be too absorbed into their own phones to hear you, or maybe it's going to be so long since they've had real human contact that they won't even know what to do. Yet I challenge you. Have a conversation with someone you are with on a queue, then see how it goes. Odds are, you will have a positive interaction, which will stick with you for the rest of the day. Most people actually enjoy chit-chatting at the store with strangers.

A lot of people get a great boost in mood from even the smallest such encounters. No matter how great it seems to feel when you get a new message or a like on your Facebook post, it will never feel the same as real interactions between humans.

So, do yourself a favor and encourage yourself to communicate at least once a week with someone you have never met before.

Now let's concentrate on the connections with your loved ones, friends, and/or family in your life. Think of someone you find to be a good friend you have not spoken to in one week or more. What is that for?

Is this because you were busy with things at work? Busy with children? You have decided for whatever reason, that other things in your life take precedence over your friendship with this person. If you were really too busy to squeeze in a 15-minute call on your mobile phone with a friend, I would ask you to consider. Perhaps you think after work you've been too busy and just didn't make it a priority.

That is something I'd ask you to improve your attitude. Relationships between one another and friendships are one of the most important aspects of our lives and it would be a disappointment to lose precious time with these people every single night of the week for a night of Netflix and pizza. I know the work is boring and you just want to come home and watch TV and forget the world. But we have also spoken about that. Why would you be wasting your life this way? If your job is so exhausting you can't focus on anything else and you're so desperate to get away from it that you can't work in the evenings, perhaps it's time to reassess your career choices.

But I'll wait in a couple of minutes for us to get to the line. Right now, this week, your challenge is to fix a date to go out and meet one of your favorite friends for a chat and maybe have dinner together. Invite them to your place and schedule a meal together if you don't want to spend money. You may want to go to his or her place because their house is more quiet... that is still okay! Whatever you decide to do, it's crucial that you set your target this week to make time for a friend. This is a great habit you're going to get a lot out of. Can get much more than the Moose Tracks ice cream pint in the fridge!

STICK TO THAT JOURNAL AND TRACK YOUR PROGRESS

Journaling is a great way of calming your mind and tracking your progress. It's nice to have a written source to refer to whenever you find you need some encouragement Try to jot somethings on every day in your journal. Write down about how you feel, what problems you have recently been successful with, and how ready you are to continue. It's also a great way to be responsible for yourself. Write down what you've been motivated to do this week and write it down as soon as you've done it.

Continue, and you'll soon have some great work pages to look back on when you like you're losing steam or need a pick-me-up. Because we have all those days, and that is all right! This is a big undertaking, as I said before. And it's critical that your problems don't turn to tasks and a major source of overthinking just like those you've worked so hard to erase! Challenge yourself, but don't stress yourself too much.

Do not attempt to take every single tip at once in this chapter! I'm setting out several solutions in the hope that there will be a few that will really make you stand out as something you think will dramatically improve your everyday life and your processes of thinking. And remember, nobody changes their lives overnight!

Keep it at the back of your mind that your journal doesn't just have to be jam-packed with words. If you're someone like me that likes motivational quotes or inspirational pictures use your journal or diary as a kind of scrapbook and include photos, quotes, cartoons, even stuff like ticket stubs and greeting cards, items you may forget or throw away. Some kinds of stuff are a lot of fun to look back on and you'll be glad to have them kept later.

Eat healthier

Eat healthier not "eat healthily." make sure it in this form because there is no safer way to ruin your progress than overloading yourself with a task like changing the way you eat completely. If you're a pretty healthy eater already, this is perfect! But I would warn you and others alike not to get caught up too much in any speculation or fad in the diet that seems to eat up your Twitter and social media feeds This is yet another perfect example of letting something become a source of frustration, overthinking, tension, and feelings of failure to improve your life. Nutrition plans and marketing supplements are just as large as any other marketing technique and you should never follow a diet or nutrition plan as the nutrition's final say.

Make use of your common sense, don't eat too much food, and try to eat healthy foods than unhealthier ones. That's all you really have to worry about when it comes to feeding right now. Don't just go on an extremely low-carb diet. There's something far more important you can deal with than that.

If you wonder what a healthier eating routine looks like, I'd suggest you keep a tab of what you eat frequently. Then, take a look. Is there anything that stands out as potentially damaging? For instance, if you eat pizzas and cookies every day and find that you feel like crap, which may be a good reason for that. I am no against eating salad and quinoa daily, and everybody can make one or two small improvements to their eating habits and see a massive improvement in overall mood and efficiency. Try to reduce the intake of sugar, and eat a few more vegetables and fruits every week. That is all you have to do to get going. As with anything else, small steps will see you go further.

Exercise

It is time for the favorite healthy mind/body activity of everybody-exercise! Do not groan, now. Let's just think about it a little. Actually, you don't have to begin marathon training or buy a whole set of dumbbells for your new unscheduled home gym. I emphasized it before and I'm going to say it for almost every tip in this list —take one step at a time. You will be far more effective with your objectives when you break things down and take it one step at a time than if you try to do so many things at the same time. It's also very important to consider your personal condition and ability, particularly with exercise. Do not compare yourself to fitness stars from YouTube who do extreme workouts every single day and chug on protein shakes. It is about you and your personal development and no one else's strategy will fit perfectly with yours.

Similar to the healthy eating pattern, the first step is to look at what you're already doing and move up a step or two on the activity ladder. That is the whole thing. If you're someone who likes to work out but doesn't seem to spare the time to do it, then I'll call you out! Exercise isn't about the hours spent doing it, it's about your hard work and I'm talking about using few minutes every day for a start. When you start at zero activity then your aim is simply to think of walking or standing instead of merely sitting down. Take in a walk around the building, or go to a park and have a little walk. If you're at home, get up every hour from your desk and do something quickly to get your blood flowing a little more. It is about making small improvements. Turn those minor changes into patterns then focus on moving up another rung.

Most people think they need a more expensive gym membership to get into better shape. That is simply not true. With no equipment and a little space, there are plenty of exercises you can do at home that are very adequate for improving your overall health. If you're actually training to participate in bodybuilding competitions, you're perhaps a unique case. But most of us will see a huge improvement in mood, strength and overall health simply by converting some of that sitting time into a little workout. If you're unsure of what to do, search the internet or go on YouTube.

Activities such as squats, jogging, lay-ups, plank hold, push-ups, walking, jumping and dancing need zero equipment and can be done nearly anywhere you feel like. If you think you'd be inspired by having a partner next to you, go for it! If you think that would be more interesting, go to a group exercise class every week. The main objective is simply to add some physical activity to your routine which is more than you used to do before. Once, don't get distracted by trying to start a 30-day challenge or 5-day intense workout schedule. The priority right now is on the mind— do not clutter it back up where you have been working so hard to find clarity.

Make time for yourself regularly

This is another which can mean many different things for different people. Setting time for yourself simply means setting time aside each day to engage in an activity that will make you feel good and relaxed. The exception I'm going to recommend here is that you're not having the time for candy or junk food. Sure, chocolate makes you feel better... for a few minutes... but ultimately, developing the habit of eating inappropriately in the name of "you" time would be a terrible idea. There are definitely other, healthier options!

Do you like massages? Many people will not get a massage every single day, of course, but you may perhaps help yourself with a good massage once a month. Choose something that relieves you on a daily basis, and set aside for just half an hour or more. Even if they just take a nap! Pick up a book, light a candle, do things that make your mind clear and relax and don't stress you up. It's about relaxing but instead of replacing your day's stresses with something loud and noisy for the rest of the night, the intention is to calm your body and mind. Stretching is a good way to do that, particularly if you've been sitting all day on an office chair. Maybe you just want to have a chat over a cup of coffee with your friend or a colleague. When possible, imagine yourself on a piece of paper before selecting something that applies to you.

Have a to-do list

Many of us enjoy planning every day and that's very cool. As we begin to get obsessed about getting everything done on the list, even those items that are not important, the issue of overthinking creeps in.

Part of developing decent habits is learning when you say no to something you just don't have the right mental energy to do so when it's not necessary. If you're feeling stressed but you are taking steps towards changing your life and behavior, then it's fine if you want to pass on that work trip or that birthday ceremony of a friend you don't even know very well. If you think that your time is best spent relaxing at home or doing something you enjoy to do, then choose for yourself. You don't always have to decide to give someone your precious time and energy just because they are asking for it. In many lives, the obligation is a strong force, and many people end up feeling bad if they don't get a yes to invitations or requests all the time. But this is just another pile of clutter that builds up in your mind that contributes to overthinking. Guilt feelings and thoughts are just as strong as any other emotion, and you should protect yourself against them.

Organize your ideal to-do list. Clearly, food shopping to feed your children comes before the hedges in the front yard are cut and this chore should be on the list further down. So make a separate list of things you need to do today and tasks you need to complete this week. That will give you a little more room and relaxation to your mind. You may get to 5 or 6 things today instead of seeing a list of 20 things to do today and the rest can be scheduled for the remainder of the week as you have time and energy.

BE GRATEFUL

It's also about purifying your feelings to clear your mind of clutter. It is crucial that you gradually replace those negative feelings with positive ones as you start to get rid of clutter and negative thoughts in your mind, as well as the clutter in your environment that is related to toxic emotions. It may take effort at first and a written reminder to get you started, but ultimately the goal is to make these thoughts automatic.

To the mind, gratitude is a powerful thing. It can turn a frustrating, poor day into something that is positive and hopeful at once. Instead of dwelling on the challenges you face and the stuff you don't have, think about all the good things in your life for which you can be grateful. Even the trivial stuff.

Is this month's utility bill paid off? That is something for which we should be grateful. Do you have people who care about you and have fun spending time with you? Lots of people don't do it — so be thankful. Do clean bed sheets make your bed comfortable and soft? Look forward to tonight's sleep, and be thankful. There are a thousand reasons for feeling grateful all around you and it's important to start recognizing them every day.

Gratitude comes with lots of warm and good emotions. It also helps you to refocus your attention on what's happening right in front of you and around you right now. A lot of us get lost in worrying about the previous day or the week before or even years before... then our thoughts turn to tomorrow and what's going on this weekend and month after and next year... How often do you ever sit back and look around and feel grateful for where you are in life? That is so important and I hope that you will make this one of your main priorities as you build new decent habits in life.

DO AWAY WITH NEGATIVE INFLUENCES

This may be one of the hardest chapters and I have been waiting until this point to write about this topic because I don't want you to feel burdened. Before you get to this stage, having a little momentum will help you see clearly, now that you have taken a step back, examined your thinking processes, and started to change them by stronger, healthier habits.

The elimination of negative influences from your life involves a lot of space, which is filled with different things from individual to individual. For everyone, negative influence doesn't look the same, so again, it is crucial that you don't get caught up in comparing yours to others. No one out there is stronger than you because they're not battling with issues the same way you do. I guarantee that all those people who seem to live amazing lives on social media are facing their own personal obstacles. Just as we've previously focused on you in previous chapters, it's time to concentrate on you and pursue those obstacles that keep you off, or worse, pushing you backward.

Go ahead and get out of a few chapters back the list listing all the roots and causes of overthinking in your life. You may have stated in the past things that happened to you that you keep carrying with you, past trauma or other people's bad treatment. Perhaps you've written things like a bad boss at work, or a colleague who keeps trying to get you high with her, or clips in the social media trends that give you photos of the person you're expected to be and that's sad. Now that we have gone a few steps forward in turning overthinking into focused achievement, it's time to take a look at your life and examine how many of those bad influences are still present.

You may have removed some major sources of overthinking, tension, and negative emotions, but are there still a few in your life that weigh you down from getting your objectives? The list would look very different for each reader and I'm not trying to take a counselor's place, but you should be able to see with a clearer mind how these influences continue to cause all sorts of problems to you. Changes in these areas are up to you, but I can give you a little advice along the way.

First of all, cutting ties with something or someone who has been around and comfortable in your life for so long is never easy, even if that presence is detrimental in the end. People see what they want to see a lot of times, and avoid anything too hard. This is actually where you were at the start when you first realized that it was time to make a change.

Getting rid of your life's negative influences is extremely important for your development. It's very easy to embark on such a path, to thrive, then to fall off on the basis of the negative influences you let your life take hold of again. Self Confidence is important but it is also important not to trivialize the power and influences of other people in your life. Sometimes even the cleverest of us get fooled, whether that was a marketing scam or a lie from a person we trust. If you have someone in your life who has a negative influence on you, it may be time for a big discussion.

Having a conversation with your friend

Next, let's think about how to reach out to friends in a strong friendship we learn several times to overlook the little things about the personality or character of the individual that we may not think are ideal. No one is flawless and your relationship is more important than many of those little flaws. You might have had bad arguments and disputes, but you know that the bond you have with the friend is very solid, if your relationship has stayed through these. But sometimes, in truth, the issues we miss are much bigger than we allow them to be and need to tackle.

There are so many different kinds of negative influences that one friend may add. The goal is to decide if these negative factors hamper the progress toward becoming a happier, more productive person. If the answer is yes, as hard as accepting it may be, it may be time to have a conversation with your friend about minimizing the influence or cutting ties altogether.

That is never an easy choice to make and at first, it can hurt. But if you're giving yourself plenty of time to think about it and keep coming back to the same simple truth, it's really a good idea to move away from it.

Seek not too confrontational is the meeting The best way to address it is through the perspective of how much you admire the good times you've had with your mate, even if the conversation ends up being a tough one.

Sit down together and get to the point by clearly describing what you are trying to do in your life.

Clarify that you are making a lot of hard changes to live a better, fuller life. Explain that you have lived with the same mentality without success for so long and now it's time to remove factors that separate you from your goals.

It may not be as bad as having to cut ties with your friend absolutely. Maybe it's actually a habit or trait you need to remind your friend to stop bringing up when he or she is with you. When they continue to gossip nonstop and speak derogatory about other persons and you find that this feeds your cycle of disturbing thoughts and overthinking, then tell your friend that you no longer want to talk to him or her about those things.

Maybe it's drug abuse, alcohol abuse or some other physically harmful factor your friend continues to bring to you. In both of these cases, as long as you come from an honest and genuine position, a friend who really cares for you and your health will understand. Don't come out accusing your mate of intentionally hurting you. They may think their lifestyle works for them and have no plans to stop them. But that doesn't mean that they aren't willing to adjust their actions around you to help you achieve your goals.

Think of one more possibility. You may start talking about what you're trying to do with your life to your friend or friends, and they may light upon the idea of trying it for themselves. You may just gain a strong ally and collaborator by having an honest conversation with your friends to move down this path of clarification. Don't be afraid to talk from an open and sincere position. In return, you might simply prove to be a powerful and positive influence on their lives!

Talking to partners or loved ones

It's hard to talk to a friend about how they might adversely affect you in some way, but it's likely going to be far more difficult to talk to a loved one or partner. If you're lucky enough to be surrounded in your life by supportive, positive influences, then actually count yourself very lucky.

However, if you are experiencing any form of a toxic relationship, addressing the problem as quickly as possible is extremely important. And while dealing with a decision to cut ties with anyone close, it is important not to confuse anything fixable by addressing and interacting with issues that are not. It all has to start with clear, honest communication.

Evidence shows a large percentage of marriage issues stem from bad habits of communication.

Miscommunication can turn small misunderstandings into devastatingly painful things. If you've said or done something your partner or loved one caused you pain, maybe it was just a miscommunication on their part. For everyone, that won't be the case, but if you've had a mostly optimistic, supportive relationship with that loved one, then there's a higher probability that it's something as easy as fixing miscommunication.

Nonetheless, if you have had a long history of constant abuse in one way or another, then it is time to gather some resources and face up to the negative influence. Do not leave without a discussion, unless you are in physical danger from the current situation. If this is the case, then exiting the situation immediately is imperative.

But if it's a matter of breaking up with a partner or talking with your wife or loved one about stoping any bad habits that damage you, then your best route is to set aside a huge amount of time for some reasonable discussion. Again, it'll be very important that you don't start the discussion by being confrontational. Be frank and provide some background and context to explain why you need to speak. Confusing your loved one won't help. As with a case where you need to talk to a relative, the best policies are transparency and vulnerability.

Do not be the only one talking n all of this, give your friend or loved one an opportunity to talk and explain how he or she really feels. If the relationship has strong qualities of redemption and is worth working on, then you should end up with some sort of understanding and agreement to move forward.

CONCLUSION

Thank you for reading all this book!

Thank you for having this book completed through to the finish. Let's hope it's been insightful and able to give you all the tools you need to reach your goals whatever they may be.

The next step is to validate that you are on your way to become a stronger, fuller person every day. Check how far you have gone, and be proud! As with anything, continuity and dedication are key to success. Have belief in yourself and your ability to make the important changes to achieve your aims.

Once you've eliminated the clutter from your mind, each and every day you convert overthinking into concentrated achievement. You may have been once told, "it is easier said than done". Well, you should be delighted to learn how to do what you devote your time to do. For a long time, you had wanted to make a move. Taking the steps toward achieving your goals is something that many people cannot do.

It is moments like this, after taking a big step forward in my life that I start to think about how far I have come. Sometimes it is difficult to appreciate your success when you are in the heat of the battle and struggling every day during the beginning, middle, or even close to the end of your endeavors. There's nothing greater than moving up onto that final ladder and looking down in your wake to see all those moves completed.

You have already taken a step towards your improvement.

Best wishes!